trust only the trembling

& other poems exploring manhood

by Christian Skoorsmith

REVISED AND EXPANDED

an imprint of
independents press
seattle, wa
2022

independents press is an imprint of
WholeHealth Publishing
9451 35th Ave SW
Seattle, WA 98126
Printed in the United States by Lulu.com.

For the King of Ramparted Uruk
Has altered the unalterable way,
Abused, changed the practices.

The Epic of Gilgamesh
Trans. by Robert Temple

For Rev. Dr. Reo Leslie, Jr.,
Gregory Flynn,

for my father, and the grandfathers I never knew,
and to all the men in my life
who make things harder
and better

my thanks

Introduction

I

II

V

Introduction

In the past I have resisted the temptation to offer any extended commentary on my poetry, let alone the presumption of an "introduction" to a collection of them as a whole. This particular collection, however, seems incomplete without one.

The topic of manhood, manliness, masculinity, and even male-bodied-ness, is a touchy one these days, to say the least. I grew up (late Gen X) on the crest of a sea-change around masculinity: the toxic, patriarchal, sexist assumptions and tropes were already being dismantled, and there was a zenith of earnest consideration about what a healthy masculinity would look like. In the 90s there grew a movement among some men (then in their forties and older) who tried to talk about the situation and next steps in nuanced ways, reaching back to myths and ceremony and a reclamation of "traditional" values (when that word meant something different than the oppression of women, but recognized a difference in gender roles that fit an alleged archetypal model). This was delicate work that was easily misunderstood and mischaracterized at the time – as I did when studying it in my early 20s. I was critical of the throwback and reactionary feel of much of the mytho-poetic men's movement: it sounded like coded language for resisting women's liberation, reducing complexity, stuck in a binary, and confusing equal relationships among genders. My cocksure complaints might have been unfair.

Recently, now in my late 40s myself, I had cause to revisit those old recordings and readings, and I heard them with different ears. In many ways, the criticisms and cautions I brought up in my 20s still held, and these works certainly come out of the cultural context of North America in the 1990s and early 2000s. But there was more there that I hadn't had ears to hear when I was younger. I found myself nodding or smiling or agreeing uncomfortably often, and something in me began to shift and open.

Perhaps this would have been the case regardless. I am of an age when the inward turn is natural, and one begins to take stock and reconsider things when facing the second-half of life, when nature and the youthful narratives of our culture run out, and we find the old tools woefully inadequate for facing a new and unsettled future. I have in this same period, been in various kinds of therapy, including personal, marriage, and relationship counseling, and work on male-socialization and racism. I also recently began writing more poetry (perhaps that is related to this stage of life, who knows).

As I dialed down in earnestness on my own issues, naturally the facts of my positionality rose up: being white in a still-white-supremacist culture, being male in a still-male-dominated/privileged world, middle-class, college-educated, native English-speaker, native-born citizen, healthy-bodied, of (relatively) sound mind, and so on – the unpacking of my privilege allowed me to discover the hidden bottom in my chest of issues, assumptions, complexes, and, yes, trauma and pain, regret and sorrow, abandoned hopes, and surrendered parts of myself buried in shame or denial. If I was going to be honest with myself, I had to ask a question that I had learned so long ago was shameful and inappropriate to ask: what does it mean to be a man, this being *as a man*? So I tried to write about those struggles and discoveries – at first therapeutically for myself, but if poetry is to be more than personal journaling it must be published and read by others. For my own accountability and continued self-exploration, and admittedly with a touch of vanity, that's what I did.

In this book I have collected recent poems (some published earlier or in different versions) that constellate my experience as a male-bodied person in some way.

Readers will find several images and themes reappearing in different pieces in this volume, examined from different angles. This reflects the discursive aspect of this work.

I offer these poems in trust that you, the reader, will hear them with an ear tuned to their context: the sincere desire to be honest and insightful, to both sit with whatever is coming up *and* have an eye toward the future, reaching out for next-steps and new formation. I suppose, that's all poetry ever is or could be.

Thank you for joining me on this journey. I hope you find some resonance of your own experience in my longing, and that together we might find a meaningful understanding of what it means to be a man for this century.

Christian Skoorsmith
Seattle, WA
June 15, 2022

Editor's Note: In an attempt to visually preserve the line-breaks as much as possible, where appropriate the word(s) in excess of the line are placed right-justified on the following line of text, preceded by an ↓ arrow. Where space does not allow for this, the overflow is right-justified on its own line. For example:

destroying the well-furrowed field for more than a season
or hope for an easier year and keep on plowing ↓or two
contrasted with:
in your lungs, the creeping sighing thoughts that surprise
you
the more surprising the more truth which is dangerous

What locks itself in endurance grows rigid; sheltered
in unassuming grayness, does it feel safe?
Wait, from the distance hardness is menaced by something
      harder still.
Alas – a remote hammer is poised to strike.

Rainer Maria Rilke, Sonnets to Orpheus

I

Half-way to sleep I see the horned beast rising

Half-way to sleep I see the horned beast rising
face contorted, black eyes seeking someone or something.
I instinctively lean into the mist looking to hide
seeing nothing.

I wonder if this is some primal force after fulfillment,
manhood or mortality on the hunt,
or Ibex-headed magic happening upon me
aware of all that I have missed or mistaken

the fathers I should have had, part of me still seeking
the father I should have been, may my children forgive me
my confusion or doubt or unsteady hand
with a box full of tools I hardly know

how to use, and even lack of love some days,
emptied of meaning but still needing
breakfasts made, hair combed, homework packed
the hugs and whispered sincerities a hope declared as
                                    much

as a statement of fact, blurred in eyes still wet with sleep.
I see the beast with a man's face I do not know
but recognize as my own, darker eyes still searching.
I am not sure I want to be found wanting

or if this mist is a mirror and I am alone
in nothing.

Song of Man

I walk the poisoned arrow in my heel,
mycelial fingers reaching up from
6000 years of shame,
a lie so deep it feels like truth.

The weight of iron and fists
in my bones denser and thicker they say
by a fraction that makes all the difference,
by a fraction that makes the whole

in my heart the shape of man,
what I hope is two-million years old in me.
The grip on my hand ax,
the instant transformation of stick

to spear or club or sword
feels something rise in me,
does not want to share the flaking tools or secrets
of fire or right to tell the story.

To understand my failures are not mine, rooted
in the struggle to survive, encoded helplessly
powerful dominant right proper
the natural order of things. It feels,

I must confess, good to be on top,
king of my molehill, chief
of my tribe imagined, answers something
hidden in shadows I sense only in my shame.

It is unjust, the sacrifice
of civilization to give up on that neglected spirit
who got me here,
survived against odds and at the expense of so many

generations of cruelty uncounted
at one end of whatever pointed stick at hand or other,
some deep trodden path covered by cultivated fields
visible only in droughts when those crops die first,

the roots kept shallow, soil too poor to sustain without
our abundance we believe is not
there, invisible from the ground but under stress
and removed to the sky is terrifyingly clear.

Like Roman walls under English farms, the architecture
we had so forgotten we did not think
to look where we had been tilling
all along. And the question what to do,

the prospect of a long, laborious, unprofitable excavation
destroying the well-furrowed field for more than a season
or hope for an easier year and keep on plowing   ⁺or two,
against the threat of a dry spell inside myself, making me

build on foundations below without
understanding the structures,
end up with an outhouse over a temple or reverse
worshiping shit as if it were real. It's easy

because there is distant truth to it, though
it may not be what we think it is, I think we know.
Not the whole tale to be told,
un-alone in the unknown waves far past.

time to honor the ghastly
forces at hand, begging for reprieve.
Where is that strength, purpose, drive
to do be stand see claim not from or over but true?

I doubt and hope nonetheless and spend
my days tracing lines in fields curious
what lies under the parch marks and ancient stones and
move under my skin.   ⁺what I feel

At 47

I feel as though I've walked into a room
and forgotten what I came in for
what I was looking for, or to do.
Looking around me silent, stunned, disbelieving
for something, or distractions.
What did I intend? It is here somewhere. I know it.

I cannot leave to enter again.

the possibility I am always

What is frightening about
the possibility I am always
lovable just as I am

nothing left
to hide or be hidden from
nothing to buy or be bidden from
not without shame or even from
those places in me I dare
not go or imagine exist and even

now distract myself with words seeking
a good turn of phrase in the place of
that inward turn where the question echoes
in the emptiness, the crowded dark
of my mind seeking to set itself aside
and listen to what I have not been willing to hear
feel what I've been too busy
this first half life to feel

flying blind as a bat waiting
for the bounce of sound to reach these outstretched ears
like sails seeking wind, to navigate the unseen textures
trajectories objects of a landscape in shadow
sending my hopes into the dark
awaiting their return, love letters
I send to a future me in the waves
of sound and silences and holding out
my heart for that brutal bathing
that leaves me raw
and readying?

Forgiveness

Shedding pasts like skin
this great cloud trails behind us
our sloughed off selves traced
only by bloodhounds and wolves,
trained by approval or hunger to follow the scent,
past victories and regrets
the billion missing moments unsung, unmeasured, lost
as we course
through time like water
scouring our being of what was.
Making room for what is.

The universe conspires sometimes, echoes,

The universe conspires sometimes, echoes,
loops back on itself, eddies in the stream
stirred up from some unseen stone or gap beneath the
                                                    surface.

Differently, on this side of another lifetime lived
from my young man's ambition and bold not-knowing,
the same threads being woven now make more sense

a clearer picture forming from the patchwork.
I did my best, I only knew what I knew
which reminds me to not know everything in the
                                        unfolding lesson

only decades later could teach me, in the fumbling and
                                                    failing,
the mumbling and flailing, the grumbling and ailing,
I look back on and see with surprise a kind of dancing
                                        with possibility

and not over yet. I raise my eyebrows, unsure
what that means. I hear the old poets saying "ahah" and
one finger raised on a hand about to point   ⁺smiling

that being point enough because what more is there
to say, a shrug that does not give up or give in
is not resigned but does not seek to fight,

the way I wanted to carve my own currents,
imagined that's how it had to be, only coming to a slow
awareness that the stream goes on whether I paddle or not.

———————

And there is so much color on these time-carved canyon
so much riparian life I miss   ⁺walls,
focused on this patch of water or the next bend in the
                                                                river.

I wonder what wizened me sits smiling
on the other side of another lifetime, what he has to say
                                                with his shrug
what compassionate regret or longing will lace my heart,

sweeten my thoughts, leaning back in the company of my
                                                                mentors
seeing another generation of foolishness, as is the way,
and if he will read these lines and shake an unsteady head

or raise a finger touching a point only we can see.

For Robert Mesle

do not trust the earth under your feet

Do not trust the earth under your feet
it is softer than you think
and moves suddenly, lurching up or down
or sideways sending you reeling,
bringing down walls and bridges
roads and tombstones alike.

Don't trust the sky overhead, it is always
changing, wet windy dry dark blue red
as if driving home the point that nothing remains
the same, as if it weren't already clear with trees leaving
and graying hair and this insatiable hunger
every day I feed but every day is renewed; I do not know
sometimes where it comes from,
like wind changing directions.
I have to pay close attention to see more
than the dust in my eyes.

Do not trust the bones in your hand
they can break and are little use to you besides,
hollow spindles filled with ooze and blood,
we hide them under skin but we all know they're there
and forget them most of the time.

Do not trust the words in your mouth or the breath
in your lungs, the creeping sighing thoughts that surprise
                                                    you,
the more surprising the more truth which is dangerous.

———————

Trust only the trembling fur of a captured mouse facing
its fate in another's hand, sure of death and seeing
no way out, chewing the last of its dinner
with dark eyes wide with unknowing.

II

A Memory of Rain

One of my earliest memories is of rain, a precious
thing in Arizona where I grew, maybe why I remember
it amid all the other moments surely I was conscious.

Camping, having arrived well after sunset and even unsure
where to pitch the tent, my father left us in the car
warm and dry, we did not know what was happening

or what was taking so long, but could hear the heavy drops
on the roof of the old pinto wagon like fat fingers tapping
from a thousand outstretched pine needles above us, as he
                                        struggled

to raise a tent of sturdy canvas, making shelter in a storm
in the dark, we watched him move like magic
in and out of the headlights pointed into the wild woods.

Having little more than a picture of what it should look
and instructions no good in the dark,   *like
fumbling almost blindly,
a project that even in daylight is at least a two-person task
                                        to build.

I can imagine the language he might have used in the dark
on that sacred ground staking his claim unconvinced
                                        perhaps
of the wisdom of things. I might have fallen asleep in the
                                        wait
or perhaps time moves differently in wonder that young.

13

We were brought into the tent, sleeping bags lined up on
                                       uneven ground
like worms rising from wet earth, but orderly,
the tent only half set-up, a lean-to for the night

the rain drumming above me in the dark
the cool mystery and utter strangeness of it all
sleeping outdoors but not, in a bed but not, with everyone

but wrapped in my own interior, everything damp
but sleep was close at hand. Waking in a different world
having slid in my slumber down the bank and bag

feet wet with water pooled in the corner

the collected condensation
from warm lungs exhaling into the night.
Morning sun illuminated this Delphic Temple so carefully
                                       constructed

if unfinished, the forest floor soft and wet
the way it is after rain, the distant thunder gone,
everything so unfamiliar and yet just right.

That bivouac patch of scented earth I loved
is as part of me as any home I've ever known.

Sins of My Father (a Republican still)

I must forgive my father the sin of his associates I know
my judgment of his lack of lacking
and the comfort he found in the shoulders of violent men
who told him he was right and good and promising
purpose, whose conviction was a soothing seething
intended against infection but also texture, flavor, color
like beets boiled too long, gelatinous.

Forgive him for too rarely being what I needed
him to be, a mixed blessing, a victim
of his own unfelt feelings
when his absence was the only gift
he had to give.
He is a good man, in many respects, I know
and has his own demons clawing the inside of his skull.

Forgive myself the tears I cry at letting go.
I am also not to
blame, unweighed by his misdirected loyalties
lofting terror on others' tongues
his vision, uncorrected still my inheritance I fear
one hand so lovingly extended
the poll arm hidden but I feel
the blows to those same loving places he held,
that my children will feel
despite my best
efforts or because I am not enough
to change the world he helped, in part
that threatens them and me
made both in love and bitterness, welcome
and reproach, the old songs of grace and care
sung in tenderness at bedtimes and campfires.

I believed in dreams
which in the light of day evaporated
like dew on grass that needs deep watering at the roots
and is given unmerciful sun.

Can I hold my father's hands
and let go of what they have done?
Those same hands cultivated in me the grounded place
on which I stand, this passionate disdain
for what he declares in part he does not do
or chooses not to admit he sees, for surely he must.

Can I forgive my father's hands,
aged mirrors of my own,
the way they move the same scars,
grieve that he was not on my side
and thankful that he did not father me to need him to be?

I remember floating as a child in the gulf
on his belly, unaware
of him paddling to stay afloat
and against the tide carrying us away,
so I could rest a moment and breathe easy,
before swimming back to shore on
my own small body buoyed by the salty sea,
and let that moment be enough to redeem
us both.

Measuring Wingspan

My mother is a mystery that cannot be unfolded
while she is alive. It seems a violence
to undo the crafted crane, and why
return to a plain sheet of wrinkled paper?
It will never lie flat again.

She has been so intentional in making ends meet
doubling back from edges
so as not to make too fine a point,
with an aim to making something beautiful
if only an impression
that touches hearts the way small acts
of beauty surprise us, left behind in a person's wake,
little gifts of gratitude that point
to a moment made precious in the pointing.

She wants so much to be
an origami blessing – beautiful, precious, held,
smiled quietly at and loved for a moment
a moment alone is enough – the humility
of paper not expecting forever, making no claim
on a distant tomorrow except in reflection.
A memory lasts longer than a poem
and that's all she wants,
would be more than satisfied to be remembered
fondly, brought back to mind,
not too much to ask for, for all she has given
(too much at times).

A paper crane always leaning
as if an ear listening closely,
or perhaps a deep tiring,

or a wounding that keeps her just off center,
always righting
until she finally rests a wing on the table,
patting the tender surface as if to say
I know, it is hard, take heart,
we will not be soon.
A love language I carry in my heart.

My mother is a crane
who thinks she's made of paper
secrets close together
left in dark folds.
She does not see
what we see from shore:
her feet deep in muddy waters,
the sky reflected in her wings.

At Liberty

I dream of a cooking class
teaching my children a deep dish
of tomatoes, basil, and cheese

only remembering the dream
when I later chance to reflect
on how much I have been given,

and to the old men in my life
how ungracious I have been,
they were not human to me then

they were forces to reckon against,
to resist, to fuel the longing,
the proprioceptive pressure in pushing away,

only pushing away
what was close enough at hand,
what connection was extended,

the pulse and warmth
of real bodies, men living
their lives of pushing and pulling

and caring for me in their way.
I feel their grasping in me, for a life
well lived, true, worthy,

the contentment of deep breaths,
feeling the fine
film of sweat in the small of my back.

———————

A smile rising, having made
room for my own children's rebellion
rejection, brash, willful misunderstanding,

needful misdirection, like a magician making believe –
look here! While the real wonder happens
behind their back – and voila! The young mind

feeling this moment as all there is
the eternal solipsism of youth.
I see it now and am still fooled,

not having entirely outgrown that tender vanity
that rises too often as resentment.
I should know better. I am that

force against which they now push,
how much in common cause with the old men
hand over loving mistaken human hand

drawing on that same rope
out of wells we cannot see
and do not know the depths

but we feel together the coolness
of the dark there, the wonder at the waters
share the thirst we hardly realize in the work.

I have to put down whatever in my boyish
self-importance I carried,
whatever stick or sword or sonnet,

---

to mourn the loss of those before I
came too late to know, seeking still
the warmth they left behind on that cord,

drawing from that well
for others playing at my feet,
biting and fighting my straining ankles.

I understand the scars on my father's shins
and tear at which were mine,
that watery blurriness welling up.

Sweet sadness feeling
the rope in my hand
hope the regret is mine too.

Feeling my father's smile
and his struggle
and why he savored songs and starry nights

that reached back to his own father.
My dad in his free time now preserves an historic home
for school-children to tour on field-trips,

so those thick-bearded unhappy-looking men
glimpsed in daguerreotypes
are known, as much as they can be, as human,

and feel at liberty there.

a wind all one's own

I did not make the bed I sleep in,
but at some point where I lay
my head is my berth
at least for a time I pause
fine beads rise on coffee reflecting
indirect sun
from a mug gifted to me praising
my fathering: legendary, it says.
One of a million such cups for a million
lackluster fathers showered with smiles
for simply being there.
A sort of accomplishment I suppose
how tempting it is to not be at times.

It isn't the diapers or playing catch or laundry.
It is the sacrifice
of my own care and free thought
(a relief I gift my own folks now
beloved and out of mind).
As with my own friends who do not need me
to mind their morning routine or change of underwear;
whom I can forget and still love because I am
loved and forgotten too, I know.
With whom I meet as equals and thus
can discover myself hidden
beneath confusion busyness doubt industry.

But as Father I am archetype
and authority, and friend
and plain unembellished
person struggling
to figure out what any of it means

in moments stolen from tasks
almost incidental, if they weren't
so precious and painful, reminding me
that I am still becoming and worthy
of a care I can only give
myself
alone and in the occasional unforeseen moment
plainly honest, equals with my kids as co-conspirators,
fellow travelers sharing a stretch of road for a spell,
the magic of this half-blink in a universe expanding
enough to justify
all the effort it takes to let
go with unreasonable hope
these little ships will stay afloat
on seas out of sight of shore.
But not yet,

because I have not given them what I need,
to know how to raise a sail
and harness a patch of wind all their own,
feeling the telling resistance in the rigging and my own
hands, and understand
in order to stay right-side-up in
this topsy-turney tide-bestraddled world is
to allow oneself to be moved.
This wide world awaits us, unmerited and unrelenting
but curved
bending back on itself to give
assurance we can find our way home again, if
we need it.
These sodden shivered timbers always
here to give them berth again

---

having learned again
for all the romance and storms
strange shores and shipwrecks
repairs and refits
sunrises and sunsets far from safe harbor,
it is swabbing the deck
that preserves us,
the inglorious soft soaking with salty water
that keeps us together and tight.

My hands imperfect as they are
can offer to my children not the swab or sail or charted
but a bearing and the sturdy feel ⁺course
of the sea against their rudder,
the good sense to turn into the waves,
look out for treasured islands
among friends, lovers, charges of their own,
even quiet moments adrift alone,
and think fondly of our time together,

feeling in the distant sun or a rising rim of land
some small measure of what was given
me.

Eva at the Cape

She dragged a stick behind her
to leave a mark in the sand as she went
and was surprised to see how uneven
how bent and wandering her path had been
for walking in a straight line.

Was it her feet that betrayed her,
always seeking balance in the soft sand
needing to land like a hockey player racing
off leaving traces of wingbeats carved behind?

Or was it the shifting hourglass fodder
finally free from so many waves
longing to cling
to her feet and hair and face
eager to leap out of the black earth
before the merciless forgetting of the tide?

Or was it the stick, that hidden imp
innocent in our hands, slave to our direction,
really a master deceiver, casting
straight lines crooked, furrowing the flaky crust
as if the whole ocean were one enormous
pie tin needing crimping at the edges,
drawing scars in flesh despite the sea's
earnest healing, our desire for
immortality manifest in our dissatisfaction
encountering a world too capable of bearing
our tender footsteps, making a weapon
of our being to mark even time
even knowing
the tide will erase us all eventually,

line, stick, stepper?

Or is it something deeper still
crying out from beneath the surface
seeking cracks through which to emerge,
that in our play and idleness we glimpse
obliquely like the landing places of rainbows
but is driving us – sand, stick, hand, wandering
and revealed only in retrospect
if we care to look back
surprised and not
how unstraight it is to trace our forward motion
when all we thought we were
was taking a walk?

Leaning Out

My arm is sore after one intent
evening playing catch with my son,
so many times reaching out
to meet his throw
wild, short, uncentered, he is
still learning and so am I.

The soreness might be an injury I need
to nurse, or it might be telling me
my arms have grown too weak
and the only way to restore them is through it.

My throwing arm is fine, I can sling
these pot shots all day and hardly feel
the pain in my shoulder.
I usually only notice it when I lie
down to sleep. There are afternoons

when he and I can't seem to connect
one mitt with another.
Sometimes every loving toss lands in the center,
the sound resonating briefly down the alley
in the chambers of my heart,
off the enamel of my front teeth.

I can rub out the discomfort in months or years,
or maybe not, and that's ok.
It is a tattoo I feel when reaching out,
a remembering that I decide what is important.

The two mitts call to me now from atop the game cabinet,
spooned together, curled around the hard ball,
held close by the memory of hands.
The ball leaning out, bigger than one glove can securely
on the edge, as it were, wanting to run out and play. ⁺hold,

Elegy (of My First Death)

I found it on the fence
around the bicycle cage
next to the playground
where I went to school.

I thought at first it was a turd
left by a bird, and I tried
to imagine how it would perch
in the chain link just perfectly

to leave absentmindedly
this inglorious monument
to its having been there, done
its business, gone its way.

Young and curious, even of poop, I
looked closer my nose almost touching
to see the delicate points,
the pleasing repeating pattern.

I realized – this is no bird-shit,
flecks of seeds transported,
ridges evidence of digestion.
No feathered beast abandoned this, flown away.

This beast is still here.
Young enough to be surprised at my own remembering
the word cocoon, and to be a witness.
This natural magic – I wanted to see it all,

_____

descend within and feel the sticky wonder, know
what new beauty emerges transformed,
reborn, alive, stretching wings, taking flight,
share the same air, brother and sister.

I felt the sun-baked fence and cruel kids,
no safe place for such sacredness,
or maybe I had already picked
it off its thin rail, discovering

I could not put it back
again. In my hand it was mine,
our fates conjoined, partners
in whatever newness about to be birthed.

I carried it home, my palm curled
as much as any mother's embrace
possible between a chrysalis and a seven-year-old boy
not knowing what to do

and too late not to do something.
Brought it home to rest
in a Styrofoam cup, twigs & leaves,
a fist-full of grass grasped down to the roots for a bed.

Plastic film over the top with air holes
punched through with a pencil, fastened with a band.
I would check on it every morning and night
like a mother expecting, something in me

waiting to be born
waiting to be born, I did not know
what or when or even the how's exactly
(still a mystery to me some 40 years later).

My family was going on a trip away
and nothing had happened yet,
maybe I had killed it already, I thought,
but put fresh grass & leaves, kept it

in a cool spot, and left.
When I returned, running,
expecting no change but hoping
(no seven-year-old really expects change, after all).

It had been born, a beautiful gray moth.
Probably a common thing,
as common as babies are
only unique to their mothers.

Wings outstretched and still
at the bottom of the cup, I understood it. Born
and died in the cruel span of my absent neglect,
my meager measures for its preserve no matter.

I still imagine the horror,
having gone to sleep wild,
trusting an uncertain future and its wings,
waking in a strange cage,

captive by an unseen film,
a token leaf and stem to cling to
as it dies – of starvation? dehydration? despair?
I never captured a wild thing again.

In capturing I had killed it,
or caused it to die,
and my moth-soul laid down
next to it and cried.

My boy-hands could not feel the weight
as I took it to the shady side of the house
where no one could see
my sorrow, my shame, and laid it

at the base of a tree, where sometimes I
would play, but less and less.
The next day it was gone and I
didn't look for it again, until just now.

Adults Outside Picking Up from a Party

We drink wine getting to know each other,
and talk of heat waves in Europe,
house maintenance, school schedules,
while an orange half-moon settles into the dark
around us. Our kids play inside,
their laughter too loud and a joy
we delight in, remembering our own and looking forward
to their relationships blooming from these
rich beds of memories, seeds being the soil.

woke to fathering

I woke to fathering too slowly,
not knowing what we were, can be
at last as well and always
within whatever bosom we suckle ourselves.
Too late to ask the simple question and not
to spend the time it takes to answer.
But there is hope in the Spring
and what we can know together, each
tilling our own gardens, tending to our own soil
side by side and reveling in
what each surprise gives life to.

On Seeing Barnacles on a Whale

Imagine moving so slow
barnacles have time to grow on your skin.
Moving through liquid life
with such deliberateness, the abundant sea
attaches itself to your body.
Such depths it is impossible to fathom.
Living forehead first,
feeling the world on the sensitive place in front of your
eyes closed, always smiling, breaths so deep,   *mind.
lungs so large that whole sleeps can take
place before rising. Imagine carrying life on our backs
that do not know we are not the ground.

Marking What I Know (The Golden Ball)

Sometimes I will pick up and hold
a pencil and some paper without anything
yet to say, an act of deepest hubris or hope
a child at prayer, Icarus stealing wings,
or that time I stole my father's truck and drove
around the block at 14 too terrified
to go any further then, far enough by far
to touch something glorious, unseen, dangerous.
As a father now I'm sure my father knew, seeing
how poor the criminal minds of children are.
We need to tutor good rebellion
without them knowing yet, lest we lift the age old truth-
It only works if they believe   ↑filled lie.
it is their choice.
Swimmers across the English Channel
using tides to their favor but never give the moon any
I realize now how much more there is   ↑credit.
in playing catch with my son, reading
to my daughter, holding hands with my child as we walk.
Cliché another word for archetype.
Rebellion, obedience,
Hope, emptiness, and longing
there must be something there,
an answer unheard in the praying,
a poem in the space
between lead and wood pulp I chase
trying to capture and replace
that first felt turn of face
when I turned the keyless starter, race
myself once
round the block to end up where I was but more,
like I got away with something,

got away with something
I spend the rest of my life getting back,
something infinite in the offing
in the daring and the doffing
treasure in wolf's clothing
lost as soon as found
the difference of pretension and pretending
a prison and a playing
make believe and waking
and, it must be said, taking
the time
the time
the time, it must be said,
even if in saying it is already lost
the sharpened end
a pencil breath
that in the end
ends
marking what I know
by what I've lost.

III

Women in Me

I grew up hearing my mother
tell me about my origins, how
my conception, if not quite immaculate, was
certainly miraculous, and how the Holy
Spirit rested on her, made her smile
at my advent, so you can understand

that part of me that is ashamed
at falling short of holy, and the voice
that builds me up in my own estimation
knowing I will just as surely fail,
my mother's loving voice telling me
I am great nonetheless, she gifted me this

bifurcation, this nonsense of my own grandiosity
as an act of purest love
and in her own humility deferring
taught me a woman's greatest love
is admiration and approval even in the face of so much
unworthy of praise, never withheld
sometimes deserved, making the fine cuts

of self-recrimination even sharper
unknown splinters working their way
to the surface in surprising routes
tracing wounds like wormholes bored in wood
leaving small piles of dust and doubt
about integrity, not to mention

the love of a woman who has no interest in
lying to me, making me feel good
for things I have not done or do not deserve

whose love for me is not presupposed, necessitated
believing there is good enough in me to merit
loving, but not more thank god
I am not her child
I can rest my head in her bosom
knowing it is not mine
still my own flawed and failing self in the making
she has no misconceptions about my sanctity
is rather fond of noting exceptions in fact
whose love is freely given and a choice
our vows did not include "till death do us part"

I need my mother, her tenderness, confidence, her always
I need my lover being her own self real   ˙smile
I need to know in my deepest the love of each
and the difference.

To the Love I've Lost

With empty hands finally
at rest and full I wish
to say I am sorry I was not
the man either of us needed me
to be. Whatever scarcity in me that crowded
like suckers around the hazelnut choking
so thick and dark no one knows
where the trunk is or if it can be saved
starving unseen fruit with lack
of courage or wisdom enough to prune the wounds
so some buds could flower in the openness,
or fear that masquerades as patience
or protection that pretends at objectivity
and does not allow for fresh wounds
or old ones to heal, remains.

At that tender age meant to be
learning love to live a lifetime
we knew trauma, and I became a child needing a mother
you could not be, because you were not her and strong
enough to sit in your own grief and not be there for me
in mine so I would not let you
and I could not be the father you needed me to be
because I am not him and collapsed under the weight
of our shared disappointment. My withering retreat
forced you to expand like a sun scorching those bodies
entrusted to its care. That's no way to live.

I have no excuse to give, and only want
your happiness and mine in this one precious go-round
room enough for life abundant if we can but find
that Goldilocks porridge and bed

before the bears come home to find what was broken
and threaten that hidden secret nested in the perfect fit.
Perhaps it is inevitable, the fierce and growling loss
of what was meant to be. It always seemed unrealistic
that she survives. But that's the story
we are told as children and maybe
we tell ourselves.

Perhaps this is the secret we are not told
that for no lack of love, and perhaps in its abundance,
these things quietly go their way,
beautiful in their going and not meant to be
forever or even half that long. That we outgrow
the favorite stories of our youth, and find
that pruning requires too much of us
or cut down the limb we set out to save
to save the tree.

In the Ponderosa forest of my youth a pine was brought
the inside rotted away to dust that stung my eyes   ⭹down
as it escaped, the whole pondering pine held up
by the few remaining rings of growth embracing an
                                                    emptiness
it could not stop from growing, could not see from the
surely it felt at its departed core. Still   ⭹outside, but
it took a lot of work to bring it down
it would not give up its claim to life
and I wonder now if it would have survived
had it been left, once the cavity was opened to the air
and whatever decaying force that was eating it from
                                                    within
laid bare to the summer sun, because for all the rings
trees keep treasured deep within
they do not grow from them, but from those nearer

42

the bark, where sap runs like tears from wounds but also
protects the tender growth beneath
to grow again, and as that towering testament proved true
to me, a few strong rings can support even
outstretched arms lifting a few scant pine needles into the
light
and bark that smells of vanilla to the nose who leans close.

a muscle in your neck

You hug too intently
pull a muscle in your neck
in that moment I think it is my fault
which is a different problem I know

and that is the end of our embracing
for now and we turn
to our separate mornings
tending our separate moorings

and the little things that make our days
livable, we are at an age where
we must recover from our sleep
rejuvenate after rest as we can

connecting as we jockey for the shower
each juggling our day ahead
and needing to depend on the other
without thinking of the need to depend

and so on, a thousand mornings thus
made before waking
cisterns emptied dry by drops
a difference we cannot measure except in years.

Let me rub your neck, my love,
and in the cool evening just ours alone
offer to you not what's left
but treasure held in tender reserve.

I know there is an egg inside of me

I know there is an egg inside of me
when half the sleep I need comes before midnight

I can hear the scraping at the shell
in the merciful absence of the mind

and hold its mystery in fear and trembling
upon the dark sea waiting wonder

it comes to me in dreams I do not dream
that dream me

from the same unseen depths as you
murderous in setting free

my movements risk disturbing the sleeping woman
in my rising the ire

to remember in the morning as I must
or I will forget long before I wake

even though part of me so desperately wants to sleep
and leave whatever is quietly rested

Back Problems (I)

My low back is lately sore but only sometimes
when I'm lurched over screens
or sleep in one position too long

maybe it is my mattress
pressed too long with restless nights
or my advancing years

it aches where muscle I did not know meets bone I do not
where I cannot reach myself   ⁺feel
where I must be kneaded by my woman

Back Problems (II)

My neck is sore
tired from looking down
at screens
at dishes
at the pavement under my next step.

Where are the horizons
the distant gazes
standing tiptoe shading eyes
it is so brilliant?

Where is the work
that looks up
felling trees intent
one eye to the wind and sway

an ear to splinters
deep-breathed pauses to take in
the scope of the task
and the work to come
hands warmed, eyes furrowed
rich lines and well-earned blisters?
The welcome soreness of exceptional service,
strength enough in my own arm?

Where is The Old Man
who has felled a hundred trees
plowed a thousand fields by hand
has carried bails, bucks, children, stories, songs?

My body is an axe rusting
at the root, leaning forgotten.

I can type 160 words a minute
but can I carry 100 pounds 100 yards
and not be winded?
Do I need to?
That is the sadness.

this bed we make

In the night I wake and I have no covers.
The blankets are curled in ribboned excess
between us, or on the far side of you,
or wrapping you like salmon at market.
I do not know, of course, if in my sleep I cast
them to you seeking distant coolness, or if
you pulled them to you like a spool winding thread
but I am cold and you are bound
it is not fair, this bed we make
in our unconscious turning.

If we are to change things, one of us will have to
drag the other along, it is not nice to
be woken from a hard-fought slumber
someone stealing thunder
destroying a delicate peace siezed
out of another hard day's short night,
resist unwinding as though it were the crime.

If we are to change things, one of us will have to
hold fast their hem, vigilant but not unkind,
the occasional grace of a tug or two,
it may take many quietly warring nights
to train each other ourselves to respect each other

                                     ourselves
to claim half of this bed we make and welcome
each other at the hump we have made in the middle
recognizing this, in our sleep and waking, stillness and
making love.   ⁺shaking, is

To my wife

you deserve dahlias
springing forth from untended soil
watering themselves

you deserve immaculate drainboards
with dishes dry and put away
and cats with sanitized feet

you deserve clean children
who are appropriately rebellious
so you can be proud of their spirits
yet are mostly kind and self-governing

you deserve a husband
who writes poems by hand praising his wife
in clear and beautiful words

you deserve your back and shoulders rubbed
your arms caressed, your beauty acknowledged
by smile, word, and body
breakfast in bed

you deserve friends unfailing
who welcome you in their unkempt houses
and think nothing of yours, only eager
to spend an hour near you
you bring each other such joy

you deserve Athena and Aphrodite
to sing your songs and raise an incense shrouded statue
in your honor, your own planet to circle the heavens

you deserve this and more, much more
and us around you
are so lucky to be the ones to fall short
in giving you our days and nights
our breath sometimes sweet and softly scented,
          sometimes foul rising honest from slumber
our hands and feet for walking with
          our stomach too soft with age
our tempers and love, the thousand outrages of life
          lived as a garden growing all sorts
we don't know yet weed from loving planted seed
          but we will, and will bring you the fruit
of our time together on this earth already precious

you deserve every goodness
and we wake every day to make that happen
but will probably need help
getting the kids ready for school

19 Years

My wife is almost the age
of her mother when we married,
which is impossible – she was so matronly then
and we are still so young,
aren't we? My body has raced ahead
but I still feel green, unprepared, playing
at adult things and as often failing.

Do not tell my bones of brittleness
nor my muscles of having grown short and stiff,
nor my belly it is too large
to fit in small spaces under chairs
like a snake at play with eagles.

I am still shedding skin and growing
in the grass as life moves over my open pores.
A part of me breathes through them!
I have only just learned to unhinge my jaw
to take more in. Yes, I sleep more
but only because digestion demands so much
of me now. We leaf through pictures

in our wedding album, our first few steps
together in the dry grass where we made love
smiling and leading, eager for the celebration to follow,
your dress too formal to wear again
(except in dreams sealed in the crawlspace
for your daughter to unpack someday),
my coat too large (I would grow into
it in time). Kids at play.

_____

We are closer to the age of our parents
sitting in staged but sincere positions,
our own children's hands resting
gently on our shoulders as if our work is
done. The foolishness
of wedding photos and remembering
how far we believed we'd come
and that somehow we were different then.
Still now...

Contemplating darker things more often
holding hands with the death of things
as a matter of course, we step
married anew into every dewy day
different and still holding
the same sinewy hand,
skin a little looser, seeing veins underneath,
beautiful too for it I'm learning.
We don't have to hold on
so hard to know we're there,
against that foolishness that got us here,
only needing to look toward each other
with that eagerness again
as if escaping, as if setting out, as if
there is a secret we are discovering, as if
the party of our lives is about to begin.

IV

for a ship a treasure something

In my dreams they are searching
for a ship? for a treasure? for something
unseen in the earth or at sea
inevitably fighting among themselves
leaving one behind as they flee
and I still do not know
who they are, what they are looking for, what they fear.

I am not among them, an observer
in my own dream, picking up in the middle
of the story and waking before it is resolved.

I could get lost in the longing
the unanswered, unended desire, the treasure
buried where no marker lies
to tell us where to dig.

Even the sand collapses in grief
saying "Give up. It is not here or anywhere."
I do not know if it is a lie.

The ship sails into the sunset
high in the hull, too light I fear
to weather a storm.

Some lawn clippings are left

Some lawn clippings are left
behind despite the earnest collector
small clumps of decay unsightly
denied the decent discretion of a distant compost pile

in the green grass still rooted
in moist earth cool to the touch
electric green with morning light
noble green by mid-day

flattened fists brown and pitted
making small shelter for unseen things underneath
I hope they will go away on their own
I do not want to stoop
no one will see them today but me

each day uglier drier until I break
them apart with the toe of my shoe
hoping they have not denied sunlight too long
to the blades below
always reaching up to meet
the blades from above when I find
time to mow again

I have heard it said that grief is

I have heard it said that grief is
something one does, while depression happens
to us: great swaths of reluctance and withdrawal
like waves moving kelp back and forth, like mother's
                                  rocking rhythm
care taking one's shoulders and directing
now the kitchen, now the shower, I got you.
There is love in the permission to lay down
one's life for a while, it is a shame
we call it illness, this feeling soft like old handkerchiefs
limp and worn out, beautiful for it. This gift
we give ourselves permission to accept
that we are worthy of care, and it takes years sometimes
to realize it.

But grief is an active thing, unwelcome
but a choice, hard work masking
as resistance, wrestling like Jacob at the riverside
to the stranger for his life it feels like   ↓unyielding
this dark angel who appears in the story from nowhere
without reason, and he won't give up
so we can't let go, even when he breaks us
until he blesses us with a limp for the rest of our lives
but we see the sunrise and wet our feet in the water as we
where our family is waiting for the rest   ↓cross
of the long journey home.

Sung of My Shadow

It is curious that
a shadow sometimes follows
      sometimes goes ahead
      sometimes walks beside us
      only rarely hidden fully in our footsteps
a constant companion
      except for ageless Peter Pan
      his youth stolen away
      by never leaving it
at some early point ceases
to be fascinating for us
as if it isn't there, as if it doesn't matter,
      as if it is a known quantity
which feels true in course, after a while too familiar
to be noticed at all
such that as a grownup now I hardly see it, disappeared
this part of myself reminded

just the other day by my child
who thought it was funny they were
taller than me a pace or two behind
I remember laughing freely
at that same thing at their age

shadows being welcome, natural
worthy of curiosity as the whole natural world
myself a part
without surprise or shame
without racism, sex, economy, mistakes, regret or risk
the whole universe unfolding freely
every distinction equal, unprojected
in my wide-eyed experience and every part of it my own

58

adventure ready

but now, but now
I sigh with a heaviness too much for my age
at loss for words, having given up
at the edge of some great emptiness and unable
to see the layered beauty on the other side that
time has uncovered in what I thought was simple stone
my shadow falling steeply down
canyon walls to explore the coolness I remember there
being close to the river, out of the sun and breathing free
                                        in the delightful dim
my shadow indistinguishable from the shade below me
                                        expansive unending
or is my shadow this whole stretch and further than I can
or is it simply a dizzy hesitancy that knows   ⁺see
down there is death and more and worse

I can feel the sun on my back growing
hot on my naked scalp – this is why
old men lose their hair, so when I turn to face the sun I
the cool shade on my skin   ⁺feel
welcoming my shadow and remembering
seen or unseen he is always here
touching me close
unfolding those petals that bloom only in the dark
and are beautiful

The Difference in Rain

In the Pacific Northwest the rain is often
so fine it manifests out of thin air
generates from within, builds
beads on leaves to fall
cascading disrupting unsettling blades
below, the subtle shakes and quivers of release
and communication, the gravity of life
descending disturbing until at last the moist
earth swollen and wet receives another
surge, an undertow of longing nourished
by the confidence of rain
shallow roots fleshed in fine moss
soft underfoot, holding fast, giving way

unlike the high-desert forests of my youth
in Northern Arizona (the name elixir
in my mouth) where roots hard as rocks
grow slowly, thick bark a brittle skin
scented in vanilla and sandalwood in Spring
when sap runs in deep cuts, pouring
resin to close the gap and guard the tender
parts within, every green cell a scramble and
bitter victory won against impossible odds and yet
life happens here, adapted to the dry demands
levied by an unremitting, unrepentant, unconscious

sun in its arc and excess, the wicking wind an unseen
force on the exposed plateau (which makes cool canyon
                                                    retreats
so sweet, the darkened recesses, hidden veins of wet
red rock that emerge as if on their own from aquifers
generations in the making) – new leaves

unfold over years, knowing from a thousand droughts
and their withered buds the risk of giving
too much, too soon, the waxy reserve hardy
against intemperance and evaporation
and roots of necessity reaching deep.

Trees in Arizona rarely fall over, standing solid even
in death long past, the rigid salute a silhouetted memory
of hopes nourished and left,
while over and over in peninsular rainforests trees
regularly collapse in their own waterlogged weight
stretched out exhausted and spent, the xylem and phloem
in rapid, successive delight dissolving   ⁺xyled and phloed
into rich humus nurturing generations
hence joining the earth in her silent rejoicing again
and again with wanton lust unrelenting

an awful mystery and besotted freedom unimagined in
desiccated days and adust nights
where longevity is key, ever living for the next distant rain
assured only of hard times between. Transplant a
heavy with dense, close rings, hard-fought   ⁺Ponderosa
into the Northwest and it will still
grow slow, genetic memory from millions of years of
                                                    adaptation
preventing absorption of water freely given, day after day
for years, its flesh still hidden under peeling layers
of softly scented reserve, too easily wounded

sap petrifying (its tears an incense in some
countries, a precious stone in others, and rosin to sweeten
music in others' still), as if the only gift worth vesting
is borne of stubbornness and struggle, loss
even in the bed of abundance. It can survive

its seeds falling on soil too rich to take root
longing for a drought to justify
the loving loam and glacial till embracing
the resistant fibrous reachings mistaking
slowness for hesitation and may even so miss
the oft-extended rain and the Spring slippery with
its nature.

Whitman sits of a morning near my cabin

There is work to be done
but the early morning cries Listen!
The pileated pecker on a hollow snag cries Listen!
and I follow barefoot into the woods
where wisdom would be to stay.

Robert Bly would sit here for an hour waiting for a poem.
Thoreau would sit here for a year.
Edward Abbey would sit here for three, on and off.
Whitman would sit here for twenty years getting to know
the field hands and fauna, hearing.

Listen! says the bracken fern, I have only
one season to sing you my song.
Listen! says the salal, as I cover the paths
you made last year, I free you!
Listen! says the foxglove reaching taller
than me, to my silent sway in the summer sun.
Listen! says the grapevine, pin my branch
out of reach of the deer, I want to fruit for thee!
Listen! says the humming birds, pausing
their fighting or courting to rest on the fenceline a moment
then return to their fury.
Listen! says the small-leaf maple, you must
lean in close, my whisper is faint, my secrets near,
I do not know how long I will keep my leaves this year.
Listen! says the broad-leaf maple, I have grown branches
                                                      low
enough to hold you, you have grown tall enough to climb,
do not miss this moment, we only have years together yet!

———————

Listen! says the Doug Fir, last year I lost
my top in the storm, but look how I have grown,
my branches like arms rising in praise
still growing, still rising, more green this year
than ever! My shaded spot for reverent St. Francis
and silent Quanyin darker now, more holy,
they have become my roots, I drink from the love
of the pets buried at my feet.
Listen! Say the thrush under the huckleberries
already budding swelling fruit for Fall,
making rushing sounds in the dry leaves
like phantom footsteps of a spirit I cannot see
but I hear circumambulating me,

nothing special, blessed to be
another log in silence, a stump
in the field, a deer at rest on the edge
of the clearing
having sat long enough for the birds to emerge
digging for seeds forgotten in the grass,
still long enough for the squirrel to forget me
and silence his alarm, turn to nuts or mate,

to be off-center in this swirling, teeming chorus
of life being lived, open and unshared.
One blade of swordfern moves
in a breeze only it can feel, and waves
to me: stay awake! There is still more to see!

Solstice Reflection

The longest day happens at night
with the solstice in sleep at 4:13am
as it happens I was awake at the time
though unwilling and shuffling
eyes closed, hand on rail, counting steps
unconsciously, to the bathroom and back
into the burrowed dark of my bed
for another hour or so of tousled rest before
awakened officially by an alarm that knows nothing
of sunrises or late nights
cares nothing for dreams or tasks awaiting
holds no interest for the curious silence
of a house yet unstirred by days' doings.

Even at noon I find myself indoors waiting
upon another opportunity to see myself
mirrored in the face of another, this solar moment
asking a reflecting lunar question: why *this* person,
why *now*, what is held in precious store here for *me*?
But the tasks, the tasks they focus and drive
push me and my reflections to quieter climes
so our time together is not wasted, my efficiency a virtue
but what is lost?

My body aching for sunlight
and warmth sinking slowly past skin,
through muscle, into my bones, Winter's dark too long
this year, Spring's cold rain unrelenting, here I am
welcoming the sun inside myself, yet and yet
tomorrow will be warmer and shorter – at first just
seconds, each one precious and uncounted   ⁺shaving
until I spend my days in twilight and wish

I had stopped to store some light in my bones
for just such a cold as that. I look ahead
and see the inevitable decline, the arc of the sun falling
lower against the horizon. Today calls me
 to receive the light arms outstretched,
live into an eternity I can savor yet, and yet

I am still indoors and working toward a time
when I can walk outside, instead of walking
outside to greet the sun right now, such is the shame
of solstice and turning toward the night once more.

Waxy Weapons

When I heard the old man grew into Alzheimer's
I nodded slowly
his words didn't always make sense to me
though I knew they were beautiful.

The waxy weapons of the Oregon Grape
and Holly leaves are still sharp
even after they've turned brown
and brittle and the wax has turned to dust.

The seasons chase the summer sun,
his blazing chariot too often hidden
behind chimeric clouds, a solid coat
worn thick against winter.

The stalks of so many woodland trees
are thin and bendy, they would not
hold my weight if I climbed them,
choking each other near the roots, lacking sun on one solid
trunk.

There are patches of grass the lawn mower missed
that lay just beyond the radius
of the tethered cord and grow wild and unkempt
as the lover's white hair in the wind.

You, dear Poet, sing songs to silence
and hear them ringing; and you, Christian,
can hardly point a warm finger
at something making noise moving in the bush.

For Robert Bly

A Young Lady Alone

We came upon each other and shared a stretch of path,
just two-hundred yards or so of secluded urban forest,
a shady departure from the sunburnt severity of the city.

It was wise for you to step aside, for you to let me pass,
you the young girl and me the man-stranger,
both of us alone but not equal in our aloneness.

Your demurral was not in deference, I'm sure
we've left those days behind us where my age
or station merits any special respect, but rather

because then I am not following you.
You have eyes on me. Safer in this small wood
where we know from so many stories bad things happen

to young girls walking alone where wolves chance.
There are wild things alive in these green veins of the city,
wolves walking in men's shoes, canines bared in broad
                                                    smiles.

I do not grudge you any mistrust, the presumption of the
I am, or the thoughts you weighed to fight or flee. ⁺danger
I am just sad that we both live in a world where that is the
                                                    smart move.

Black Lives Matter

My first draft of this
poem was title and a blank page
for what more needs to be
said and who cares

what another white man has
to say about it and who am I
saying it for anyway, the only
people who will read it are those

who already agree. If those
words could read without needing
elaboration, explanation, justification,
there wouldn't be a poem after all.

A statement of plain fact does no good,
a third of White Lives will disagree,
a third will nod somberly,
another third don't care, either way.

I will leave this poem much as I was
the shame of it
the lack of it
the lees of it

and they will go on mattering no matter
what, and the ridiculous grammar of I and they
both misleading lie and deepest truth
one subject and one object leave me

---

listless in hope
of something other than myself
and to accept what I cannot
as a first unarticulate step

yet, yet, yet,
for all my introspection
my heart's deep longing fear intent
I will walk home without concern

for losing my life.

Friends I Long For

I want to sing the iron lungs in my life
in slow, deep, sincere tones too rarely sung,
those dear friends who have met me
in my weakness and shallow breaths
not knowing what I did not know
or could take in or let go
who have with alternating pressure and ease have helped
me breathe deeper than my soul-sickened diaphragm was
                                        prepared for.
Bly, Whitman, Rilke, the greats, and also the few
men who asked questions that would not let me wriggle
                                        off the hook,
that could not be answered black and white,
yes or no, leaving talk of business or weather
to the crows feeding on roadsides,
who invited me to dig underneath
and left the space open for me to sit in the hole
I had dug and weep.

I have not yet emerged from that earth
or shaken the soil from my clothes,
but I have found roots there extending
from the walls left by my scraping and stretching
me in those directions. Your patience in
my darkness is a sacred trust I feel
the strength around me, the solid walls
of your earnestness and accountability
your opening and faithing
the rhythm reminding my heart to breathe.

Sandplay

Did you know, I ask, conscious
of my lilting voice wanting
to convey curiosity and breeze
the way fish-ticklers are patient,

there are neurons in you seeking
neurons in me so we both know how to feel,
excited or alert or in love?
So a part of us unknown

is guiding us to hold hands with each other,
to sync souls. We need so much,
our hearts born lonely.
We will give up so much

to be a part of something more, lose our minds
to feel found; we can't help it.
In love, in violence, even in rebellion,
and in quiet moments,

where our deepest skin wears thin straining against a scar,
discover what we've known for too long,
allowed the sudden hurt that has been to be,
as in my mothers containing hands,

or the forgiving sand below the tide line.
To know the feeling as neither the enemy
nor the task, but an open door.

Where are the violins I hear in my head

Where are the violins I hear in my head
when everything is quiet? Where are the zealots
in my chest that keep me up at night?

Where are the wounds that cause my lips to fall asleep,
and what are the needles I feel as they wake?
What are the hummingbirds at my window as my wife
                                        plays Spanish guitar?

What are the flesh-eating worms in my gut at 2AM,
and why are they so thirsty?
Why are there so few shadows at night?

What is left after all the questions?
When we are exhausted and finally do not wish
to fight anymore?

Where is the boy, his thumb, and the dike?
Will it matter he does not come home or is lost at sea?
There are no elegies written for him; only legends of those
                                who did not listen to him.

Where are the arias I compose in my sleep?
The tender loosings I hear as I wake?
They do not sing to me.

In the end, Christian, you are nothing:
an empty drum, a bell big enough to fit your head into,
that space inside a guitar no one ever sees.

The pipe of my youth lies lonely, unsmoked

The pipe of my youth lies lonely, unsmoked.
The tins of tobacco still tucked away
in softening boxes stored on shelves in the garage.

Seeing them suddenly I long for the quiet
nights and solitary, soulful ceremony,
the time it takes to pack a bowl and tamp it down at the
edges.

A corn cob from those years of deliberateness
rests enshrined in a bowl on a shelf like a relic,
an unbelievable, common thing, pointing to something

uncommon, unbelievable unless you'd been there
to see the small flame transformed by loving breath
into sacred bathwater connecting me

with the moon, the pine trees, and the open
spaces between. How many nights
trespassing back from something sacred,

lost like smoke in silent, howling hymns
to all this – this world, my body, this moment –
with a slowness that took the time to take?

A fine pipe my mother bought me
and my father's favorite tobacco blend
from a shop that no longer exists
in a town where now only the memory of our hearts live,

_____

echo muted hymns of hope every time I touch it, by

surprise

coming upon it while rummaging in a drawer
for something else – longing to feel

the warmth of my hand and the glow
of a fire in the belly. I always think:
later.

I tuck it back, intently,
still smelling the sacred, feeling
the *temenos* I knew then,

and have tamped down now at the edges.

What Passes Underneath Between Us

The city sends a reminder about resident responsibilities
for side sewers – those connections
between the common pipe and individual
homes, carrying the secrets we all share, including
our tendency to ignore them unless there is
a problem, when our effluence leaks
and the grass grows too ripe, the earth slippery
with what we'd rather not revisit.

A defining quality of civilization, this gift
of imagining there is nothing so unpleasant within us,
that there is no downstream,
that we are clean inside and out,
our garbage disappearing weekly at the street,
whatever grime we've collected or created for ourselves
washed away in scented cascades of too much
water, our swirling muck vanishing
while we wash our hands,
returning without mention to the dinner party.

We pass off so much
and let go of so little,
seeking containers for the contents
of our bowels, the dark soft foulness
we carry and deposit
in small poisons all over the earth,
as likely to disappear as footsteps
in ancient clay, leaving an empty space
where we were, to witness our passing.

I hope there is earth enough
a thousand generations hence, to wonder innocently
what passed through their distant forebears,
their side sewers connecting them
out of sight, out of mind,
allowing them the fantasy of independence.

Niawiakum River

the river flows slow and wide here
with years between bends
where the broad bed is broached
with grass and one never quite knows
if the bank is being built up or eroded
by its going

Too long with broken shells

Even the man in a house on fire
can spare a few moments
for a cat that climbs on his lap.

Towels not moved by the wind
dry brittle and scratchy
folding them feels like breaking something.

The dark huckleberry outside my window shakes
too much and too long until a squirrel manages
to emerge as if from quicksand

reach a low-hanging limb
and dance among branches bouncing
with seeds about to be let go.

Chickens will learn to eat their own eggs
if left too long with broken shells,
the corruption of generations in captivity.

Christian, how long will you hold
the pencil hoping genius
strikes from that feeling, red-glowing iron on the anvil?

V

What Does It Mean (to be a man)?

I can feel the hew of the ax in my hands but
there are too few fires to justify splitting so much
wood and too few rounds to pull from forests
of trees felled by fungus creeping unchecked for years
through the roots, a rot passed along
in the soil. What does it mean
to be something I am embarrassed to admit
I am? That I want more of what I can't understand?
Want more but cannot understand what I
want more of and not more?

my naked body. The sunlight

These trees have lived a hundred years to praise
my naked body. The sunlight has traveled 93 million miles
to rest on my tender parts. This grass grown roots
to bear me reverently above the earth   ˙gathering green
spinning its massive self eager to show me a radiant sky.
                                        The whole
universe erupting from the head of a pin, the cosmos an
                                              acrobat
performing for me this moment infinitely singular.
It would be abominable not to open the gift, as if
I am the leading edge of the universe knowing itself,
as if I at this moment am all that matters and am not me
but everything.
It would be a blasphemy to ask what it is or if
it is true. My being a prayer.

around these ancient flames burning

Being told of one's cruelty is a poison
one must take to die well
and keep the retching resistance close
enough to see it clearly.
The toxins I've been drinking daily
and dishing in so many quiet ways,
I told myself the kids could not hear
or even was my job as a father,
embracing some model of contingent love
pointing to the exiled parts of my own heart
still unhealed, even unknown, hinted at
in disapproval or the tired sigh of my
projected exhaustion. I remember feeling their
feelings, speaking almost their words, in their position
and they are not wrong just as I was,
met with that same wounding
cuts bleeding through generations,
an inherited hemophilia that cannot stay
the wounds and risks
bleeding out, each drop a cutting edge.

Even now the safety of metaphor allows
a distant reflection to break up
like sunlight on water, I squint and turn
my hand rising to shield my eyes against
the bitter blinding light against
the dark red back of my eyes
a ghost there moving unseen
except for the blindspot it leaves.

Plainly, I have hurt,
and in my flailing I have hurt

and am still flailing myself.
I must sink without knowing
if there is anything I can do or cannot do,
anything that can be done or undone,
my knees in the ash of a thousand fires,
my hair wreaking of smoke
so thick I hardly smell it anymore,
my hands weary from another night's harried dance
around these ancient flames burning
everything inside me. I do not know
if there is enough water in the world to quiet
these smoldering coals. I wait at the edge
of the Pacific Ocean and trust there
are tears enough for everyone in the tide.

a float sailing these seas

Among the treasures along the coast
is a glorious graveyard of buoys and lines
rescued from the sea – strange shapes still strong
with silent stories to tell
of work and chance, lives lost and found, did they fear
the drifting? were they missed? what
teeth mistook them for prey? are there still
eyes that scan the sea for them or are they
lost, orphaned, escaped, adventurous? would they rather
in the waves again circling the wide globe,   ⁺be
like whales horrifically stranded but with no eyes
wet with fear to plead for a push
or a saltwater bath between tides?
My soul feels like that sometimes, I know the look.
Or, impossible, are they proud somehow
to companion campsites, hang from trees
to hold food bags from predators and varmints,
sway in the wind like chimes ringing too deep to hear,
and envy the lucky few who find strong limbs
and the untethered imagination of children swinging,
their laughter a float sailing these seas?

To That Just Beyond My Steps

It takes a long time to get to know
a patch of field, a square yard

of real earth, years in fact
watching, tending, listening,

fretting over warm winters that threaten
dry summer days

noting the softly favored paths
of white tail deer who know
where the sweet grass is

stooping to pull invasive broom
before it goes to seed

it takes a lot of quiet days
that should have been spent elsewhere
more productive, more ROI, it takes

care to see it by lit by moonlight
and wet with darkness in welcome storms

a patch I belong to as much as it belongs
to me in the final accounting

the pair of us close enough to hold hands
for the briefest of walks in each others' company

and I miss it, that wild garden far removed from the city
miss my weight on soil that changes over seasons yet
remains

a friend who every week apart grows
its own way, soon strangers to each other

until we have enough time to sit again
allowing each to be again

holding each other in the hope and unknowing
and the moment
as if we were brothers all along.

A Story for My Children

My children ask me if I have any regrets – what do I give
Courage? My own baggage? I rummage through   ᵗthem?
memories like fingers in a Rolodex
of shame I keep at the ready,
in a dark space for late nights and after too many drinks.

A story of a kitten who needed me
when I was in college, but I could not
keep, the terms of my lease being unfriendly,
so I left it in the snowstorm where I found it.
I do not know what became of it
or the part of me left out
on the counter to be so callous.
I can't imagine it survived
that cold Iowa winter, but
I do not know.
Sometimes I can still hear it
crying at my closed door.

But it can be driven

It is easier, it is written, for a camel
through the eye of the needle than a rich man
to enter heaven, because the camel need only kneel
and be unburdened, inch on its knees
like a child making tracks in sand
and it merely does not want to;
it is not in its nature.

Tall House (Wupatki)

There is a place near my childhood
where the earth breathes. I was surprised
how small her mouth is,

how long her inhales and exhales.
I never did sit for a whole breath. I feel
the shortness of breath in my own small lungs.

The earth breathes for us or
in spite of us, amid the ruins
and faded footsteps of people long passed.

A longing part of me loves them
as I circle their crumbling homes
the slow breaths of my steps
I think of my own walls

just out of reach. She goes on breathing
in a desert the colors of ruins.

There is a fragile glory rising

There is a fragile glory rising
early, meeting the sunrise
with coffee and a book already
in hand, Spring warm
enough for bare feet but cool
enough to be alone

with the birds and squirrels in morning song,
the tit-mouse and junko and far off
a murder of crows playing counterpart
in animated staccato to a train's long vowel,
the distant river of people
rushing already to important things
resigned, I imagine, or hope a few are dancing
in their seat-belts to some private joy.

I with a moment
to notice and breathe in the cool
clouded sky increasingly bright
on the other side of the cedar
as gold filters higher through the sad branches smiling,
a brilliance I imagine but

the growing shades of green on this side more
than enough radiance for the moment
to be more than enough to read by,
this book of impossible poetry
opened before me.

What thou lovest well remains,
the rest is dross

Ezra Pound

About the Author

Christian Skoorsmith lives and works in Seattle, Washington, as a father, husband, gardener, bagpiper, and hypnotherapist. Christian was raised in Northern Arizona, attended university in the Midwest, and has lived and worked in Western and Eastern Europe, before relocating to the Pacific Northwest. When not in the city, he can be found carving an off-grid homestead on Harstine Island with his family. This collection brings together material written in 2022 reflecting his positionality as a male-socialized/male-identifying person. Christian also regularly contributes to two professional hypnosis journals and speaks nationally and internationally on hypnotherapy-related topics.